PRAYER JOURNAL

THE
POWER
OF A
Praying®
Woman

STORMIE
OMARTIAN

HARVEST HOUSE™ PUBLISHERS

EUGENE, OREGON

Cover by Koechel Peterson & Associates, Inc., Minneapolis, Minnesota

THE POWER OF A PRAYING® WOMAN PRAYER JOURNAL
Copyright © 2002 by Stormie Omartian
Published by Harvest House Publishers
Eugene, Oregon 97402

ISBN 0-7369-0542-1

Printed in the United States of America.

02 03 04 05 06 07 / DC-MS / 10 9 8 7 6 5 4 3 2 1

Welcome to a life of prayer...

Writing in a journal is one of the best things you can do for yourself. It's therapeutic, in fact. It causes you to think clearly about what the deepest desires of your heart are. It helps you to round up and anchor your thoughts and put them in a letter to the Lord. Writing out your prayers can be as powerful as speaking them, and it is a great way to communicate deeply with your heavenly Father. Plus, it is faith building to record the answers to your prayers as they manifest. Every time you go back and read what you have written, you will see all that God has done in your life, and you will be encouraged to pray even more. I invite you to put all of your burdens and cares on these pages. Leave them in God's hands, where they belong.

—*STORMIE OMARTIAN*

*It is your Father's good pleasure to give you
the kingdom.*

—LUKE 12:32

Lord, I long to dwell in Your presence,
and my desire is for a deeper and more
intimate relationship with You. I want
to know You in every way You can be
known. Teach me what I need to learn
in order to know You better. Teach me
to pray the way You want me to. Help
me to learn more about You. Lord, You
have said, "If anyone thirsts, let him
come to Me and drink" (John 7:37). I
thirst for more of You because I am in a
dry place without You. I come to You
this day and drink deeply of Your Spirit.

Prayer Journal

The Power of a Praying Woman

Prayer Journal

_____
_____
_____
_____
_____
_____
_____
_____
_____
_____
_____
_____
_____
_____
_____
_____
_____
_____
_____
_____
_____
_____
_____
_____
_____

...teach me to pray

Until now you have asked nothing in My name. Ask, and you will receive, that your joy may be full.

—JOHN 16:24

Lord, I know You are everywhere, but I also know that there are deeper manifestations of Your presence that I long to experience. Draw me close so that I may dwell in Your presence like never before. I am open to whatever You want to do in me. I don't want to limit You by neglecting to acknowledge You in every way possible. I declare this day that You are my Healer, my Deliverer, my Redeemer, and my Comforter. Today I especially need to know You as (put in a name of the Lord). I believe You will be that to me.

Prayer Journal

_____
_____
_____
_____
_____
_____
_____
_____
_____
_____
_____
_____
_____
_____
_____
_____
_____
_____
_____
_____
_____
_____
_____
_____
_____
_____
_____

Prayer Journal

_____

_____

_____

_____

_____

_____

_____

_____

_____

_____

_____

_____

_____

_____

_____

_____

_____

_____

_____

_____

_____

_____

_____

_____

_____

_____

_____

_____

...my Redeemer and Comforter

He who covers his sins will not prosper, but whoever confesses and forsakes them will have mercy.

—Proverbs 28:13

Lord, forgive me for thoughts I have had, words I have spoken, and things that I have done that are not glorifying to You or are in direct contradiction to Your commands. I know that You are "gracious and merciful, slow to anger and of great kindness" (Joel 2:13). Forgive me for ever taking that for granted. I realize that You are a God who "knows the secrets of the heart" (Psalm 44:21). Show me any place in my life where I harbor sin in my thoughts, words, or actions that I have not recognized. Show me the truth about myself so that I can see it clearly.

Prayer Journal

_____

_____

_____

_____

_____

_____

_____

_____

_____

_____

_____

_____

_____

_____

_____

_____

_____

_____

_____

_____

_____

_____

_____

_____

_____

_____

_____

_____

...show me the truth about myself

Repent therefore and be converted, that your sins may be blotted out, so that times of refreshing may come from the presence of the Lord.

—Acts 3:19

Lord, I pray that You will "have mercy upon me, O God, according to Your lovingkindness; according to the multitude of Your tender mercies, blot out my transgressions. Wash me thoroughly from my iniquity, and cleanse me from my sin" (Psalm 51:1-2). "Create in me a clean heart...and renew a steadfast spirit within me. Do not cast me away from Your presence, and do not take Your Holy Spirit from me" (Psalm 51:10-11). Make me clean and right before You. Enable me to make changes where I need to do so. I want to receive Your forgiveness so that times of refreshing may come from Your presence.

Prayer Journal

Prayer Journal

_____
_____
_____
_____
_____
_____
_____
_____
_____
_____
_____
_____
_____
_____
_____
_____
_____
_____
_____
_____
_____
_____
_____
_____
_____

...create in me a clean heart

Love your enemies, bless those who curse
you, do good to those who hate you, and
pray for those who spitefully use you and
persecute you, that you may be sons of your
Father in heaven.

—MATTHEW 5:44-45

Lord, help me to understand the depth
of Your forgiveness toward me so that I
won't hold back forgiveness from others.
I realize that forgiving someone doesn't
make them right; it makes me free. You
are the only one who knows the whole
story, and You will see justice done.
Expose the recesses of my soul so I
won't be locked up by unforgiveness.
Please remind me to pray for those who
hurt or offend me so that my heart will
be soft toward them. I don't want to
become hard and bitter because of
unforgiveness. Make me a person who
is quick to forgive.

Prayer Journal

_____
_____
_____
_____
_____
_____
_____
_____
_____
_____
_____
_____
_____
_____
_____
_____
_____
_____
_____
_____
_____
_____
_____
_____
_____
_____
_____
_____

...forgiveness makes me free

Honor your father and your mother, that
your days may be long upon the land which
the LORD *your God is giving you.*

—EXODUS 20:12

Lord, show me if I have any unforgiveness toward my mother or father. I don't
want to shorten my life by not honoring
them and breaking this great commandment. And where there is distance
between me and any other family mem-
ber because of unforgiveness, I pray You
would break down that wall. Help me
to forgive every time I need to do so. I
know I cannot be a light to others as
long as I am walking in the darkness of
unforgiveness. Where I can be an instrument of reconciliation between other
family members who have broken or
strained relationships, enable me to do
that.

Prayer Journal

The Power of a Praying Woman

Prayer Journal

...break down that wall

Whatever we ask we receive from Him,
because we keep His commandments and do
those things that are pleasing in His sight.

—1 JOHN 3:22

Lord, my heart wants to obey You in all things. Show me where I am not doing that. If there are steps of obedience I need to take that I don't understand, I pray You would open my eyes to see the truth and help me to take those steps. I know I can't do all things right without Your help, so I ask that You would enable me to live in obedience to Your ways. Help me to hear Your specific instructions to me. Your Word says that those who love Your law will have great peace and nothing will cause them to stumble (Psalm 119:165).

Prayer Journal

Prayer Journal

...obey You in all things

Take up the whole armor of God, that you
may be able to withstand in the evil day,
and having done all, to stand.

—EPHESIANS 6:13

Lord, show me when I am not recogniz-
ing the encroachment of the enemy in
my life. Teach me to use the authority
You have given me to see him defeated
in every area. Reveal to me any place in
my life where I am walking in disobedi-
ence. If I have given the enemy a place
in my protective armor through which
he can secure a hook, show me so I can
rectify it. Gird me with strong faith in
You and in Your Word. Help me to fast
and pray regularly in order to break any
stronghold the enemy is trying to erect
around me.

Prayer Journal

Prayer Journal

...gird me with strong faith

*The Lord is faithful, who will establish you
and guard you from the evil one.*

—2 Thessalonians 3:3

Lord, thank You that by the power of
Your Holy Spirit I can successfully resist
the devil and he must flee from me
(James 4:7). You are my shield because I
live Your way (Proverbs 2:7). Help me
to "not be overcome by evil," but
instead give me the strength to "overcome evil with good" (Romans 12:21).
Hide me in the secret place of Your presence from the plots of evil men (Psalm
31:20). Thank You that even though the
enemy tries to take me captive to do his
will, You have given me the power to
escape his snares completely (2 Timothy
2:26).

Prayer Journal

Prayer Journal

_____

_____

_____

_____

_____

_____

_____

_____

_____

_____

_____

_____

_____

_____

_____

_____

_____

_____

_____

_____

_____

_____

...You are my shield

To be carnally minded is death, but to be
spiritually minded is life and peace.

—ROMANS 8:6

Lord, Your Word is "a discerner of the thoughts and intents of the heart" (Hebrews 4:12). As I read Your Word, may it reveal any wrong thinking in me. May Your Word be so etched in my mind that I will be able to identify a lie of the enemy the minute I hear it. Spirit of truth, keep me undeceived. I know You have given me authority "over all the power of the enemy" (Luke 10:19), and so I command the enemy to get away from my mind. Thank You, Lord, that I "have the mind of Christ" (1 Corinthians 2:16). I want Your thoughts to be my thoughts.

Prayer Journal

Prayer Journal

_____

_____

_____

_____

_____

_____

_____

_____

_____

_____

_____

_____

_____

_____

_____

_____

_____

_____

_____

_____

_____

_____

_____

_____

_____

...I have the mind of Christ

You will keep him in perfect peace, whose mind is stayed on You, because he trusts in You.

—Isaiah 26:3

Lord, I don't want to give place to thoughts that are not glorifying to You. I don't want to walk according to my own thinking (Isaiah 65:2). I want to bring every thought captive and control my mind. Show me where I have filled my mind with anything that is ungodly. Help me to resist doing that and instead fill my mind with thoughts, words, music, and images that are glorifying to You. Help me to think upon what is true, noble, just, pure, lovely, of good report, virtuous, and praiseworthy (Philippians 4:8). I lay claim to the "sound mind" that You have given me (2 Timothy 1:7).

Prayer Journal

Prayer Journal

_____
_____
_____
_____
_____
_____
_____
_____
_____
_____
_____
_____
_____
_____
_____
_____
_____
_____
_____
_____
_____
_____
_____
_____
_____

...bring every thought captive

*If anyone desires to come after Me, let him
deny himself, and take up his cross daily, and
follow Me. For whoever desires to save his life
will lose it, but whoever loses his life for My
sake will save it.*

—LUKE 9:23-24

Lord, I love You with all my heart, with all my soul, and with all my mind. I commit to trusting You with my whole being. I declare You to be Lord over every area of my life today and every day. Enable me to deny myself in order to take up my cross daily and follow You. I want to be Your disciple just as You have said in Your Word (Luke 14:27). I want to lose my life in You so I can save it (Luke 9:24). Teach me what that means. Speak to me so that I may understand.

Prayer Journal

The Power of a Praying Woman

Prayer Journal

_..._ _I love You with all my heart_

Trust in the LORD *with all your heart, and lean not on your own understanding; in all your ways acknowledge Him, and He shall direct your paths.*

—PROVERBS 3:5-6

Lord, help me to say yes to You immediately when You give me direction for my life. I surrender myself to You and invite You to rule in every part of my mind, soul, body, and spirit. I declare this day that "I have been crucified with Christ; it is no longer I who live, but Christ lives in me; and the life which I now live in the flesh I live by faith in the Son of God, who loved me and gave Himself for me" (Galatians 2:20). Rule me in every area of my life, Lord, and lead me into all that You have for me.

Prayer Journal

Prayer Journal

...I surrender myself to You

Whoever keeps His word, truly the love of
God is perfected in him. By this we know
that we are in Him.

—1 JOHN 2:5

Lord, Your Word is food to my soul,
and I can't live without it. Enable me to
truly comprehend its deepest meaning.
Give me greater understanding than I
have ever had before, and reveal to me
the hidden treasures buried there. I pray
that I will have a heart that is teachable
and open to what You want me to
know. Help me to be diligent to put
Your Word inside my soul faithfully
every day. Give me the ability to memorize it. Etch it in my mind and heart.
Make it become a part of me. Change
me as I read it.

Prayer Journal

_____
_____
_____
_____
_____
_____
_____
_____
_____
_____
_____
_____
_____
_____
_____
_____
_____
_____
_____
_____
_____
_____
_____
_____
_____
_____
_____

Prayer Journal

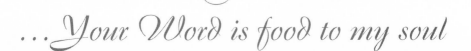

... Your Word is food to my soul

He who heeds the word wisely will find good,
and whoever trusts in the LORD, *happy is he.*

—PROVERBS 16:20

Lord, I don't want to be just a hearer of
Your Word. Show me how to be a doer
of Your Word as well. Help me to apply
my heart to Your instruction and my
ears to Your words of knowledge
(Proverbs 23:12). May Your Word correct my attitude and remind me of what
my purpose is on earth. May it cleanse
my heart and give me hope that I can
rise above my limitations. May it
increase my faith and remind me of who
You are and how much You love me.
May it bring the security of knowing my
life is in Your hands.

Prayer Journal

Prayer Journal

...apply my heart

All of you be submissive to one another, and
be clothed with humility, for "God resists the
proud, but gives grace to the humble."

—1 PETER 5:5

Lord, please give me a submissive heart. Help me to submit to governing authorities and the correct people in my family, work, and church. Show me who the proper spiritual authorities are to be in my life. Plant me in the church You want me to be in. Help me to move into proper alignment in every area of my life by willingly submitting myself to others where I need to do so. Give me discernment and wisdom about this. I seek You first this day and ask that You would enable me to put my life in perfect order.

Prayer Journal

The Power of a Praying Woman

Prayer Journal

_____

_____

_____

_____

_____

_____

_____

_____

_____

_____

_____

_____

_____

_____

_____

_____

_____

_____

_____

_____

_____

_____

_____

_____

_____

...give me a submissive heart

Offer to God thanksgiving, and pay your
vows to the Most High. Call upon Me in the
day of trouble; I will deliver you, and you
shall glorify Me.

—PSALM 50:14-15

Lord, thank You that You are "gracious
and full of compassion, slow to anger
and great in mercy" (Psalm 145:8).
Thank You that You are "mighty in
power" and Your "understanding is infi-
nite" (Psalm 147:5). Thank You that
You execute justice for the oppressed,
You give food to the hungry, and You
give freedom to the prisoners. Thank
You that You open the eyes of the blind
and raise up those who are bowed down
(Psalm 146:7-8). Thank You, Lord, that
You have a future for me that is full of
hope. Thank You that You are always
restoring my life to greater wholeness.

Prayer Journal

Prayer Journal

_____
_____
_____
_____
_____
_____
_____
_____
_____
_____
_____
_____
_____
_____
_____
_____
_____
_____
_____
_____
_____
_____
_____
_____
_____
_____

...gracious and full of compassion

But the hour is coming, and now is, when the true worshipers will worship the Father in spirit and truth; for the Father is seeking such to worship Him.

—JOHN 4:23

Lord, I exalt Your name, for You are great and worthy to be praised. Thank You that "You have put gladness in my heart" (Psalm 4:7). All honor and majesty, strength and glory, holiness and righteousness are Yours, O Lord. I praise Your name this day, for You are good, and Your mercy endures forever (Psalm 136:1). "Because Your lovingkindness is better than life, my lips shall praise You. Thus I will bless You while I live; I will lift up my hands in Your name" (Psalm 63:3-4). May praise and worship of You be my first response to every circumstance.

Prayer Journal

_____

_____

_____

_____

_____

_____

_____

_____

_____

_____

_____

_____

_____

_____

_____

_____

_____

_____

_____

_____

_____

_____

_____

_____

_____

_____

_____

_____

_____

_____

Prayer Journal

_____

_____

_____

_____

_____

_____

_____

_____

_____

_____

_____

_____

_____

_____

_____

_____

_____

_____

_____

_____

_____

_____

_____

_____

_____

_____

_____

...great and worthy to be praised

Do you see a man who excels in his work?
He will stand before kings; he will not stand
before unknown men.

—PROVERBS 22:29

Lord, Lord, whatever it is You have called me
to do, both now and in the future, I
pray You will give me the strength and
energy to get it done well. Thank You
that in all labor there is profit of one
kind or another (Proverbs 14:23). Bless
the people I work for and with. May I
always be a blessing and a help to each
one of them. As I come in contact with
others in my work, I pray that Your love
and peace will flow through me and
speak loudly of Your goodness. Enable
me to touch them for Your kingdom.

Prayer Journal

The Power of a Praying Woman

_...bless the people
I work for and with_

Every man should eat and drink and enjoy
the good of all his labor; it is the gift of God.

—ECCLESIASTES 3:13

Lord, teach me to excel so that the result
of what I do will be pleasing to others.
Open doors of opportunity to use my
skills and close doors that I am not to
go through. Give me wisdom and direction about that. I commit my work to
You, Lord, knowing You will establish it
(Proverbs 16:3). May it always be that I
love the work I do and am able to do
the work I love. According to Your
Word I pray that I will not lag in diligence in my work, but remain fervent in
spirit, serving You in everything I do
(Romans 12:11).

Prayer Journal

Prayer Journal

_____
_____
_____
_____
_____
_____
_____
_____
_____
_____
_____
_____
_____
_____
_____
_____
_____
_____
_____
_____
_____
_____
_____
_____
_____
_____
_____
_____
_____

...open doors of opportunity

I am the vine, you are the branches. He who abides in Me, and I in him, bears much fruit; for without Me you can do nothing.

—JOHN 15:5

Lord, You are the vine and I am the branch. I must abide in You in order to bear fruit. Help me to do that. Thank You for Your promise that if I abide in You and Your Word abides in me, I can ask what I desire, and it will be done for me (John 15:7). Thank You for Your promise that says if I ask I will receive (John 16:24). May I be like a tree planted by the rivers of Your living water so that I will bring forth fruit in season that won't wither (Psalm 1:3).

Prayer Journal

Prayer Journal

...bring forth fruit in season

Therefore, having these promises, beloved, let
us cleanse ourselves from all filthiness of the
flesh and spirit, perfecting holiness in the fear
of God.

—2 CORINTHIANS 7:1

Lord, I know I have been washed
clean and made holy by the blood of
Jesus (1 Corinthians 6:11). You have
clothed me in Your righteousness and
enabled me to put on the new man
"in true righteousness and holiness"
(Ephesians 4:24). Continue to purify
me by the power of Your Spirit.
Help me to "cling to what is good"
(Romans 12:9) and keep myself pure
(1 Timothy 5:22). Give me discernment to recognize that which is
worthless and remove myself from it.
Help me not to give myself to impure
things, but rather to those things that
fulfill Your plans for my life.

Prayer Journal

Prayer Journal

_____

_____

_____

_____

_____

_____

_____

_____

_____

_____

_____

_____

_____

_____

_____

_____

_____

_____

_____

_____

_____

_____

_____

_____

_____

...I have been washed clean

In a great house there are not only vessels of gold and silver, but also of wood and clay, some for honor and some for dishonor. Therefore if anyone cleanses himself from the latter, he will be a vessel for honor, sanctified and useful for the Master, prepared for every good work.

—2 TIMOTHY 2:20-21

Lord, I want to be holy as You are holy. Make me a partaker of Your holiness (Hebrews 12:10), and may my spirit, soul, and body be kept blameless (1 Thessalonians 5:23). Show me how to tear down any idols in my life and eliminate any sources of unholy thoughts, such as TV, movies, books, videos, and magazines, that do not glorify You. Help me to examine my ways so that I can return to Your ways wherever I have strayed. Thank You that You will keep me pure and holy so I will be fully prepared for all You have for me.

Prayer Journal

Prayer Journal

_____

_____

_____

_____

_____

_____

_____

_____

_____

_____

_____

_____

_____

_____

_____

_____

_____

_____

_____

_____

_____

_____

_____

_____

_____

...help me examine my ways

Walk worthy of the calling with which you were called, with all lowliness and gentleness, with longsuffering, bearing with one another in love, endeavoring to keep the unity of the Spirit in the bond of peace.

—EPHESIANS 4:1-3

Lord, I thank You that You have called me with a holy calling, not according to my works, but according to Your purpose and grace which was given to me in Christ Jesus (2 Timothy 1:9). Take away any discouragement I may feel and replace it with joyful anticipation of what You are going to do through me. Use me as Your instrument to make a positive difference in the lives of others. Help me to rest in the confidence of knowing that Your timing is perfect. I know that whatever You have called me to do, You will enable me to do it.

Prayer Journal

Prayer Journal

_____

_____

_____

_____

_____

_____

_____

_____

_____

_____

_____

_____

_____

_____

_____

_____

_____

_____

_____

_____

_____

_____

_____

_____

*...You have called me
with a holy calling*

You are a chosen generation, a royal priest-hood, a holy nation, His own special people, that you may proclaim the praises of Him who called you out of darkness into His mar-velous light.

—1 PETER 2:9

Lord, I put my identity in You and my destiny in Your hands. Show me if what I am doing now is what I am supposed to be doing. I want what You are building in my life to last for eternity. I don't want to presume that I know what Your plan is. Nor do I want to spend a lifetime trying to figure out what I am supposed to be doing and miss the mark. So I pray that You would show me clearly what the gifts and talents are that You have placed in me. Lead me in the way I should go as I grow in them.

Prayer Journal

The Power of a Praying Woman

_____

_____

_____

_____

_____

_____

_____

_____

_____

_____

_____

_____

_____

_____

_____

_____

_____

_____

_____

_____

_____

_____

_____

_____

_____

_____

_____

_____

...I put my identity in You

A new commandment I give to you, that you love one another; as I have loved you, that you also love one another. By this all will know that you are My disciples, if you have love for one another.

—JOHN 13:34-35

Lord, I release all my relationships to You and pray that Your will be done in each one of them. With my most difficult relationships, I ask that Your peace would reign in them. Specifically, I lift up to You my relationship with (name a difficult friend). I know two can't walk together unless they are agreed (Amos 3:3), so help us to find a place of agreement, unity, and like-mindedness. Where either of us needs to change, I pray that You would change us. I ask that You would make our relationship what You want it to be so that it will glorify You.

Prayer Journal

The Power of a Praying Woman

Prayer Journal

_____
_____
_____
_____
_____
_____
_____
_____
_____
_____
_____
_____
_____
_____
_____
_____
_____
_____
_____
_____
_____
_____
_____
_____
_____
_____
_____
_____
_____

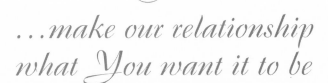

*...make our relationship
what You want it to be*

Ointment and perfume delight the heart, and the sweetness of a man's friend gives delight by hearty counsel.

—Proverbs 27:9

Lord, I pray for my relationships with friends and family members. I ask You to bless each one. I pray You would bring healing, reconciliation, and restoration where it is needed. Bless all of my relationships and make them strong. Help me to be a good friend, sister, cousin, daughter, aunt, niece, granddaughter, and prayer supporter. I pray for godly friends, role models, and mentors to come into my life. Send people to me who will speak the truth in love. I pray especially that there will be women in my life who are trustworthy, kind, loving, and faithful. Help me to be Your light in all my relationships.

Prayer Journal

Prayer Journal

_____

_____

_____

_____

_____

_____

_____

_____

_____

_____

_____

_____

_____

_____

_____

_____

_____

_____

_____

_____

_____

_____

_____

_____

_____

_____

_____

_____

...bless all my relationships

The world is passing away, and the lust of it;
but he who does the will of God abides forever.

—1 John 2:17

Lord, You are more important to me than anything. Your will is more important to me than my desires. I want to live as Your servant, doing Your will from my heart (Ephesians 6:6). Align my heart with Yours. If I am doing anything outside of Your will, show me. Speak to me from Your Word so that I will have understanding. Show me any area of my life where I am not right on target. If there is something I should be doing, reveal it to me so that I can correct my course. I want to do only what You want me to do.

Prayer Journal

The Power of a Praying Woman

Prayer Journal

_____
_____
_____
_____
_____
_____
_____
_____
_____
_____
_____
_____
_____
_____
_____
_____
_____
_____
_____
_____
_____
_____
_____
_____
_____
_____
_____
_____

...align my heart with Yours

He shall give His angels charge over you, to
keep you in all your ways.

—PSALM 91:11

Lord, I want to dwell in Your secret
place and abide in Your shadow (Psalm
91:1). Help me never to stray from the
center of Your will or off the path You
have for me. Send Your angels to keep
charge over me and keep me in all my
ways. May they bear me up, so that I
will not even stumble (Psalm 91:12).
You, Lord, are my refuge and strength
and "a very present help in trouble."
Therefore I will not fear, "even though
the earth be removed and though the
mountains be carried to the midst of the
sea" (Psalm 46:1-2).

Prayer Journal

_____

_____

_____

_____

_____

_____

_____

_____

_____

_____

_____

_____

_____

_____

_____

_____

_____

_____

_____

_____

_____

_____

_____

_____

_____

_____

_____

_____

_____

_____

_____

Prayer Journal

_____
_____
_____
_____
_____
_____
_____
_____
_____
_____
_____
_____
_____
_____
_____
_____
_____
_____
_____
_____
_____
_____
_____
_____
_____
_____
_____
_____

...my refuge and strength

You shall not be afraid of the terror by night,
nor of the arrow that flies by day, nor of the
pestilence that walks in darkness, nor of the
destruction that lays waste at noonday. A
thousand may fall at your side, and ten thou-
sand at your right hand; but it shall not come
near you.

—PSALM 91:5-7

Lord, I ask that You would keep me safe in planes, cars, or any other means of transportation. Keep me from sudden danger. "Be merciful to me, O God, be merciful to me! For my soul trusts in You; and in the shadow of Your wings I will make my refuge" (Psalm 57:1). I trust in Your Word, which assures me that You are my rock, my fortress, my deliverer, my shield, my stronghold, and my strength in whom I trust. Thank You that "I will both lie down in peace, and sleep; for You alone, O Lord, make me dwell in safety" (Psalm 4:8).

Prayer Journal

_____
_____
_____
_____
_____
_____
_____
_____
_____
_____
_____
_____
_____
_____
_____
_____
_____
_____
_____
_____
_____
_____
_____

...You make me dwell in safety

If you cry out for discernment, and lift up
your voice for understanding, if you seek her
as silver, and search for her as for hidden
treasures; then you will understand the fear of
the LORD, *and find the knowledge of God.*
For the LORD *gives wisdom; from His mouth*
come knowledge and understanding.

—PROVERBS 2:3-6

Lord, I pray You would increase my wisdom and knowledge so I can see Your truth in every situation. Help me to always seek godly counsel and not look to the world and ungodly people for answers. Thank You that "You will show me the path of life" (Psalm 16:7-11). I delight in Your law and in Your Word. Help me to meditate on it day and night, to ponder it, to speak it, to memorize it, to get it into my soul and my heart. I know that whoever "trusts in his own heart is a fool, but whoever walks wisely will be delivered" (Proverbs 28:26).

Prayer Journal

Prayer Journal

_____
_____
_____
_____
_____
_____
_____
_____
_____
_____
_____
_____
_____
_____
_____
_____
_____
_____
_____
_____
_____
_____
_____
_____

...You will show me
the path of life

The fear of the LORD is the beginning of wisdom, and the knowledge of the Holy One is understanding. For by me your days will be multiplied, and years of life will be added to you.

—Proverbs 9:10-11

Lord, thank You that You give "wisdom to the wise and knowledge to those who have understanding" (Daniel 2:21). I seek discernment for each decision I must make. Help me to walk uprightly, righteously, and obediently to Your commands. May I never be wise in my own eyes, but may I always fear You. Keep me far from evil so that I can claim the health and strength Your Word promises (Proverbs 3:7-8). Give me the wisdom, knowledge, understanding, direction, and discernment I need to keep me away from the plans of evil so that I will walk safely and not stumble (Proverbs 2:10-13).

Prayer Journal

The Power of a Praying Woman

Prayer Journal

_____

_____

_____

_____

_____

_____

_____

_____

_____

_____

_____

_____

_____

_____

_____

_____

_____

_____

_____

_____

_____

_____

_____

_____

_____

_____

...so I will walk safely

The LORD shall help them and deliver them;
He shall deliver them from the wicked, and
save them, because they trust in Him.

—PSALM 37:40

Lord

Lord, I know that I can't see all the ways the enemy wants to erect strongholds in my life. I depend on You to reveal them to me. Thank You that You came to "proclaim liberty to the captives and recovery of sight to the blind, to set at liberty those who are oppressed" (Luke 4:18). Without You I am held captive by my desires, I am blind to the truth, and I am oppressed. But with You comes freedom from all that. "My times are in Your hand; deliver me from the hand of my enemies, and from those who persecute me" (Psalm 31:15).

Prayer Journal

The Power of a Praying Woman

_____

_____

_____

_____

_____

_____

_____

_____

_____

_____

_____

_____

_____

_____

_____

_____

_____

_____

_____

_____

_____

_____

_____

_____

_____

_____

_____

_____

_____

_____

Prayer Journal

...with You comes freedom

The righteous cry out, and the LORD *hears,*
and delivers them out of all their troubles.

—PSALM 34:17

Lord, I know that "we do not wrestle
against flesh and blood, but against
principalities, against powers, against
the rulers of the darkness of this age,
against spiritual hosts of wickedness in
the heavenly places" (Ephesians 6:12).
Thank You that You have put all these
enemies under Your feet (Ephesians
1:22), and "there is nothing covered that
will not be revealed, and hidden that
will not be known" (Matthew 10:26).
Make darkness light before me and the
crooked places straight (Isaiah 42:16). I
call upon You, Lord, and ask that You
would deliver me from anything that
binds me or separates me from You.

Prayer Journal

_____

_____

_____

_____

_____

_____

_____

_____

_____

_____

_____

_____

_____

_____

_____

_____

_____

_____

_____

_____

_____

_____

_____

_____

_____

...make darkness light before me

Then they cried out to the LORD *in their trouble,*
and He saved them out of their distresses. He
brought them out of darkness and the shadow
of death, and broke their chains in pieces.

—PSALM 107:13-14

Lord, thank You that in my distress I
can call on You. And when I cry out to
You, Lord, You hear my voice and
answer (Psalm 18:6). You have said in
Your Word that by our patience we can
possess our souls (Luke 21:19). Give me
patience so that I can do that. Help me
to keep my "heart with all diligence,"
for I know that "out of it spring the
issues of life" (Proverbs 4:23). Help me
to not miss opportunities to focus on
You and extend Your love to those
around me. May the joy of knowing
You fill my heart with happiness and
peace.

Prayer Journal

The Power of a Praying Woman

...You hear my voice and answer

Wait on the LORD; *be of good courage, and He shall strengthen your heart; wait, I say, on the* LORD!

—PSALM 27:14

Lord, no matter what dark clouds settle on my life, I believe You will lift me above them and into the comfort of Your presence. Only You can take whatever loss I experience and fill that empty place with good. Only You can take away the burden of my pain. "Hear me when I call, O God of my righteousness! You have relieved me in my distress; have mercy on me, and hear my prayer" (Psalm 4:1). I want to have hope in the midst of difficult times and not surrender to hopelessness. Thank You that I walk before You with hope in my heart and life in my body.

Prayer Journal

Prayer Journal

_____

_____

_____

_____

_____

_____

_____

_____

_____

_____

_____

_____

_____

_____

_____

_____

_____

_____

_____

_____

_____

_____

_____

_____

_____

_____

_____

...hear me when I call

Beloved, do not think it strange concerning
the fiery trial which is to try you, as though
some strange thing happened to you; but
rejoice to the extent that you partake of
Christ's sufferings, that when His glory is
revealed, you may also be glad with exceeding
joy.

—1 Peter 4:12-13

Lord, remind me that You have
redeemed me and I am Yours and nothing is more important than that. I know
when I pass through the waters You will
be with me and the river will not over-
flow me. When I walk through the fire I
will not be burned, nor will the flame
touch me (Isaiah 43:1-2). That's because
You are a good God and have sent Your
Holy Spirit to comfort and help me. I
pray that You, O God of hope, will fill
me with all joy and peace and faith so
that I will "abound in hope by the
power of the Holy Spirit" (Romans
15:13).

Prayer Journal

The Power of a Praying Woman

Prayer Journal

_____
_____
_____
_____
_____
_____
_____
_____
_____
_____
_____
_____
_____
_____
_____
_____
_____
_____
_____
_____
_____
_____
_____
_____
_____
_____

...You have redeemed me

*Let us lay aside every weight, and the sin which so
easily ensnares us, and let us run with endurance
the race that is set before us, looking unto Jesus,
the author and finisher of our faith, who for the
joy that was set before Him endured the cross,
despising the shame, and has sat down at the right
hand of the throne of God.*

—HEBREWS 12:1-2

Lord, do not allow me to be led into
temptation, but deliver me from the evil
one and his plans for my downfall.
Keep me strong and able to resist anything that would tempt me away from
all You have for me. I pray I will have
no secret thoughts where I entertain
ungodly desires to do or say something
I shouldn't. I pray that I will have no
secret life where I do things I would be
ashamed to have others see. Thank You
that You hear my cries and will save me
from any weakness that could lead me
away from all You have for me (Psalm
145:18-19).

Prayer Journal

The Power of a Praying Woman

_____
_____
_____
_____
_____
_____
_____
_____
_____
_____
_____
_____
_____
_____
_____
_____
_____
_____
_____
_____
_____
_____
_____
_____

...You hear my cries
and will save me

*"I will restore health to you and heal you of
your wounds," says the* LORD.

—JEREMIAH 30:17

Lord, I look to You for my healing
whenever I am injured or sick. I pray
that You would strengthen and heal me
today. Heal me "that it might be fulfilled
which was spoken by Isaiah the prophet,
saying: 'He Himself took our infirmities
and bore our sicknesses' " (Matthew
8:17). You suffered, died, and were
buried for me so that I might have healing, forgiveness, and eternal life. By
Your stripes I am healed (1 Peter 2:24). I
know that in Your presence is where I
will find rest and refreshment. In Your
presence I can reach out and touch You
and in turn be touched by You.

Prayer Journal

Prayer Journal

_____
_____
_____
_____
_____
_____
_____
_____
_____
_____
_____
_____
_____
_____
_____
_____
_____
_____
_____
_____
_____
_____
_____
_____
_____
_____

...strengthen and heal me

Confess your trespasses to one another, and
pray for one another, that you may be healed.
The effective, fervent prayer of a righteous
man avails much.

—JAMES 5:16

Lord, You have said in Your Word, "My
people are destroyed for lack of knowledge" (Hosea 4:6). I don't want to be
destroyed because I lacked knowledge of
the right thing to do. Teach me and help
me learn. Lead me to people who can
help or advise me. Enable me to follow
their suggestions and directions. When I
am sick and need to see a doctor, show
me which doctor to see and give that
doctor wisdom as to how to treat me. Be
Lord over every part of my life so that I
can bring my life into alignment with
Your will.

Prayer Journal

Prayer Journal

_____

_____

_____

_____

_____

_____

_____

_____

_____

_____

_____

_____

_____

_____

_____

_____

_____

_____

_____

_____

_____

_____

_____

_____

_____

_____

_____

...be Lord over my life

There is no fear in love; but perfect love casts out fear.

—1 John 4:18

Lord, guard my heart and mind from the spirit of fear. What I am afraid of today is (name anything that causes you to have fear). Take that fear and replace it with Your perfect love. If I have any thoughts in my mind that are fueled by fear, reveal them to me. If I have gotten my mind off of You and on my circumstances, help me to reverse that process so that my mind is off my circumstances and on You. Show me where I allow fear to take root and help me to put a stop to it. Replace this fear with the fear of the Lord.

Prayer Journal

The Power of a Praying Woman

Prayer Journal

...perfect love casts out fear

The fear of the Lord is a fountain of life, to
turn one away from the snares of death.

—Proverbs 14:27

Lord, I know You have not given me a
spirit of fear, so I claim the power, love,
and sound mind You have for me. "Oh,
how great is Your goodness, which You
have laid up for those who fear You"
(Psalm 31:19). Thank You that "the fear
of the Lord leads to life, and he who has
it will abide in satisfaction; he will not
be visited with evil" (Proverbs 19:23).
Help me to grow in fear and reverence
of You so I may please You and escape
the plans of evil for my life. Thank You
that those who fear You will never lack
any good thing.

Prayer Journal

The Power of a Praying Woman

Prayer Journal

...how great is Your goodness

Most assuredly, I say to you, he who believes
in Me, the works that I do he will do also;
and greater works than these he will do,
because I go to My Father. And whatever you
ask in My name, that I will do, that the
Father may be glorified in the Son. If you ask
anything in My name, I will do it.

—John 14:12-14

Lord, reveal to me any area of my life
where I should be giving to someone
right now. I don't want to get so
wrapped up in my own life that I don't
see the opportunity for ministering Your
life to others. Help me to make a big
difference in the world because You are
working through me to touch lives for
Your glory. Show me what You want me
to do and enable me to do it. Give me
all I need to minister life, hope, help,
and healing to others. Make me to be
one of Your faithful intercessors, and
teach me how to pray in power.

Prayer Journal

Prayer Journal

_____

_____

_____

_____

_____

_____

_____

_____

_____

_____

_____

_____

_____

_____

_____

_____

_____

_____

_____

_____

_____

_____

_____

_____

_____

_____

_____

_____

_____

_____

...teach me how to pray in power

My heart is overflowing with a good theme; I recite my composition concerning the King; my tongue is the pen of a ready writer.

—PSALM 45:1

Lord, help me to speak only about things that are true, noble, just, pure, lovely, of good report, virtuous, and praiseworthy. "Let the words of my mouth and the meditation of my heart be acceptable in Your sight, O Lord, my strength and my Redeemer" (Psalm 19:14). May every word I speak reflect Your purity and love. Your Word says that "the preparations of the heart belong to man, but the answer of the tongue is from the Lord" (Proverbs 16:1). I will prepare my heart by being in Your Word every day so that the words I speak can come from You.

Prayer Journal

The Power of a Praying Woman

Prayer Journal

...I will prepare my heart

The heart of the wise teaches his mouth, and adds learning to his lips.

—PROVERBS 16:23

Lord, fill my heart with Your love, peace, and joy so that they will flow from my mouth. Convict me when I complain or speak negatively. Help me not to speak too quickly or too much. I pray You would give me the words to say every time I speak. Give me words that testify of the hope within me. Help me know when to speak and when to be silent. And when I do speak, give me words to say that will bring life and encouragement. Help me to be a woman who always speaks wisely, graciously, and clearly and never foolishly, rudely, or carelessly.

Prayer Journal

Prayer Journal

...give me words that bring life

Lord, I know that "faith comes by hearing, and hearing by the word of God" (Romans 10:17). Make my faith increase every time I hear or read Your Word. Help me to believe for Your promises to be fulfilled in me. Give me strength to stand strong on them and believe Your every word. I pray that the genuineness of my faith, which is more precious than gold that perishes even when it is tested by fire, will be glorifying to You, Lord (1 Peter 1:7). Make my faith large so I can pray in power. Increase my faith daily so I can move mountains in Your name.

Prayer Journal

Prayer Journal

_____

_____

_____

_____

_____

_____

_____

_____

_____

_____

_____

_____

_____

_____

_____

_____

_____

_____

_____

_____

_____

_____

_____

_____

...increase my faith daily

*"My grace is sufficient for you, for My strength is made perfect in weakness."
Therefore most gladly I will rather boast in my infirmities, that the power of Christ may rest upon me.*

—2 Corinthians 12:9

Lord, I know I can't change myself in any way that is significant or lasting, but by the transforming power of Your Holy Spirit all things are possible. Where I am resistant to change, help me to trust Your work in my life. Grant me, according to the riches of Your glory, to be strengthened with might through Your Spirit in my inner being (Ephesians 3:16). May Your love manifested in me be a witness of Your greatness. May Your light so shine in me that I become a light to all who know me. May it be not I who lives, but You who live in me (Galatians 2:20).

Prayer Journal

*...help me to trust
Your work in my life*

Brethren, I do not count myself to have apprehended; but one thing I do, forgetting those things which are behind and reaching forward to those things which are ahead, I press toward the goal for the prize of the upward call of God in Christ Jesus.

—PHILIPPIANS 3:13-14

Lord, help me to let go of anything I have held on to of my past that has kept me from moving into all You have for me. Enable me to put off all former ways of thinking and feeling and remembering (Ephesians 4:22-24). Give me the mind of Christ so I will be able to understand when I am being controlled by memories of past events. I don't want to tie myself to the past by neglecting to forgive any person or event associated with it. I release my past to You and everyone associated with it so You can restore what has been lost.

Prayer Journal

Prayer Journal

_____

_____

_____

_____

_____

_____

_____

_____

_____

_____

_____

_____

_____

_____

_____

_____

_____

_____

_____

_____

_____

_____

_____

_____

_____

…I release my past to You

Let your eyes look straight ahead, and your eyelids look right before you. Ponder the path of your feet, and let all your ways be established.

—PROVERBS 4:25-26

Lord, everything that was done to me or I have done that causes me pain, I surrender to You. May it no longer torment me or affect what I do today. Make me glad according to the days in which I have been afflicted and the years I have seen evil (Psalm 90:15). Thank You that You make all things new and You are making me new in every way (Revelation 21:5). Help me to keep my eyes looking straight ahead and not back on the former days and old ways of doing things. I know You want to do something new in my life today.

Prayer Journal

Prayer Journal

_____

_____

_____

_____

_____

_____

_____

_____

_____

_____

_____

_____

_____

_____

_____

_____

_____

_____

_____

_____

_____

_____

_____

...You make all things new

*Surely goodness and mercy shall follow me all
the days of my life; and I will dwell in the
house of the* LORD *forever.*

—PSALM 23:6

Lord, I don't want to be trying to secure
my future with my own plans. I want to
be in the center of Your plans, knowing
that You have given me everything I
need for what is ahead. I pray You
would give me strength to endure without giving up. You have said that "he
who endures to the end will be saved"
(Matthew 10:22). Help me to run the
race in a way that I shall finish strong
and receive the prize You have for me
(1 Corinthians 9:24). I put my future in
Your hands and ask that You would give
me total peace about it.

Prayer Journal

Prayer Journal

_____
_____
_____
_____
_____
_____
_____
_____
_____
_____
_____
_____
_____
_____
_____
_____
_____
_____
_____
_____
_____
_____
_____
_____
_____
_____

...I put my future in Your hands

Arise, shine; for your light has come! And the glory of the LORD is risen upon you. For behold, the darkness shall cover the earth, and deep darkness the people; but the LORD will arise over you, and His glory will be seen upon you.

—ISAIAH 60:1-2

Lord, I know Your thoughts toward me are of peace, to give me a future and a hope (Jeremiah 29:11). I know that You have saved me and called me with a holy calling, not according to my works, but according to Your own purpose and grace (2 Timothy 1:9). I humble myself under Your mighty hand, O God, knowing that You will lift me up in due time. I cast all my care upon You, knowing that You care for me and will not let me fall (1 Peter 5:6-7). I want to walk with You today into the future You have for me.

Prayer Journal

Prayer Journal

...the future You have for me